DANCE FUN

by Cari Meister

PEBBLE
a capstone imprint

Pebble Emerge is published by Pebble, an imprint of Capstone.
1710 Roe Crest Drive, North Mankato, Minnesota 56003
www.capstonepub.com

Library of Congress Cataloging-in-Publication Data
Names: Meister, Cari, author.
Title: Dance fun / by Cari Meister.
Description: North Mankato : Capstone Press, [2021] | Series: Sports fun | Includes bibliographical references and index. | Audience: Ages 6-8 | Audience: Grades 2-3 | Summary: "Dance is fun to watch, but it's even more fun to do! Kids can take the stage by learning what dance is, what gear and skills are needed, what happens during lessons, and how to be a good sport. A special activity helps kids build a basic dance skill"-- Provided by publisher.
Identifiers: LCCN 2020037723 (print) | LCCN 2020037724 (ebook) | ISBN 9781977132277 (hardcover) | ISBN 9781977154064 (pdf) | ISBN 9781977155771 (kindle edition)
Subjects: LCSH: Dance--Juvenile literature.
Classification: LCC GV1596.5 .M45 2021 (print) | LCC GV1596.5 (ebook) | DDC 792.8--dc23
LC record available at https://lccn.loc.gov/2020037723
LC ebook record available at https://lccn.loc.gov/2020037724

Image Credits
iStockphoto: adamkaz, 21, Alfa Studio, cover (boy); Shutterstock: A_Lesik, 17, Africa Studio, 11, AlenKadr, 9, antoniodiaz, 14, BAZA Production, 12, bissun, 10, DenisProduction.com, 8, Flamingo Images, 7, FXQuadro, 15, Iakov Filimonov, 5, 18, Jianbing Lee, 6, Lucia Polko (stars), cover, back cover, 1, Maria Symchych, 16, SFROLOV, 19, tsaplia (speakers), cover, back cover, 1, Vereshchagin Dmitry, 13, Wiktoria Matynia (notes), cover, back cover, 1

Editorial Credits
Editor: Jill Kalz; Designer: Tracy McCabe; Media Researcher: Eric Gohl; Production Specialist: Katy LaVigne

Printed and bound in the USA. PO 3837

TABLE OF CONTENTS

Words in **bold** are in the glossary.

WHAT IS DANCE?

Dancing is fun! When you dance, you move your body. You may move fast or slowly. You may move only parts of your body or all of you!

There are many kinds of dance. Each kind has different moves or steps. **Ballet**, **ballroom**, **tap**, and **hip-hop** are a few kinds of dance. Most are done to music.

Dance often tells a story. It may tell a light, happy story. It may tell a sad, angry, or scary story. Dancers use their faces and bodies to tell the stories. They may leap, twirl, or stomp. They may spin on their heads!

WHAT DO I NEED?

Bare feet are OK for some kinds of dance. For others, you need special shoes. Ballet shoes are soft and fit close to your feet. Ballroom shoes have a low or high **heel**.

metal soles

Tap shoes have metal pieces on their
soles. The metal makes *tap-tap-tap* sounds
when you dance. Dance sneakers are good
shoes for hip-hop. They hold on to the floor.

Dancers wear light clothing that lets them move easily. Some wear a **leotard** and tights. Some wear a dress or skirt. Others wear a T-shirt, shorts, or stretchy pants. Close-fitting clothes are good for ballet. They make it easy to see a dancer's **posture**.

WHERE DO I LEARN?

Many places have dance classes. Some schools and fitness centers have classes. People may teach dance in their homes. There are also special dance schools.

Dance classes are held in large, open spaces. Students need room to move. The walls may have big mirrors. Seeing how your body moves helps you learn.

HOW DO I LEARN?

Before you dance, you warm up. You stretch. You get loose. Then you learn dance steps. You learn how to move your feet, arms, and body the right way.

Your teacher will ask you to do the
same steps many times. Practice makes
you stronger. You might learn the steps
without music first.

It can take a long time to dance well. Going to class is important. But it's just as important to practice on your own too.

One day, you and your class may put on a dance show. You may wear costumes and makeup. It's fun to show your family what you have learned!

HOW CAN I BE A GOOD SPORT?

Keep dance fun by being a good sport. Go to class ready to work hard. Listen to your teacher. Be kind to other dancers.

Help others if they need it. Let them help you too. If you have a bad day, it's OK. Do your best and keep dancing!

SKILL BUILDER: GOOD POSTURE

Your posture is the way you hold your body when you stand or sit. A dancer needs good posture. Try these things to make your posture better.

- Sit tall in a chair and pull in your stomach. Hold for a count of five and repeat.

- Place a book on your head. Keep your chin level and try walking without the book falling off.

- Stand tall with your back against a wall. Push your shoulders down and back until they touch the wall. Pull in your stomach so your lower back touches the wall too.

Check yourself in a mirror. Do you look strong and tall?

GLOSSARY

ballet (ba-LAY)—a form of dance with set steps and movements that is light and graceful

ballroom (BALL-room)—a set of partnered dances with set steps; examples are the waltz and tango

heel (HEEL)—the back part of a person's foot, below the ankle

hip-hop (HIP-hop)—a form of high-energy street dance usually done to hip-hop music

leotard (LEE-uh-tard)—a snug, one-piece bodysuit worn by dancers and gymnasts

posture (POSS-chur)—the way the body is held when sitting or standing

sole (SOHL)—the bottom of a person's foot

tap (TAP)—a form of dance with set steps that uses special shoes with metal pieces on the soles

READ MORE

Lee, Laura. *A Child's Introduction to Ballet: The Stories, Music, and Magic of Classical Dance.* New York: Black Dog & Leventhal, 2020.

Singer, Marilyn. *Feel the Beat: Dance Poems That Zing from Salsa to Swing.* New York: Dial Books for Young Readers, 2017.

INTERNET SITES

Basic Ballet Positions
https://www.pbt.org/learn-and-engage/resources-audience-members/ballet-101/basic-ballet-positions/

Dance Facts for Kids
https://kids.kiddle.co/Dance

INDEX